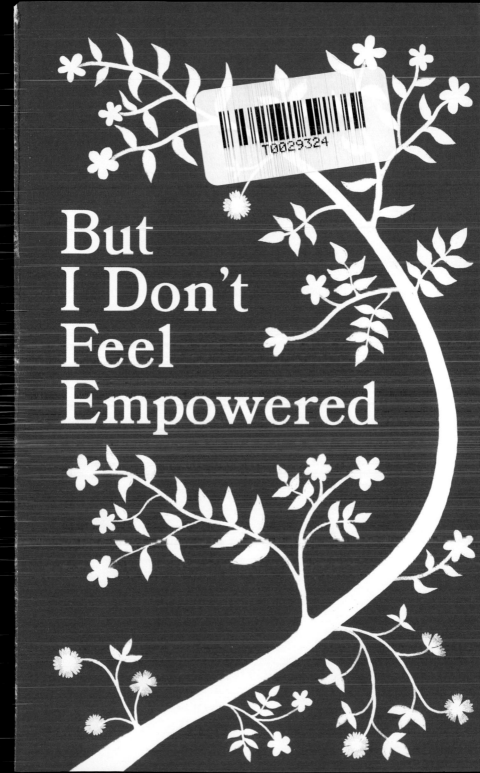

But I Don't Feel Empowered

But I Don't Feel Empowered

Suri Chan

Andrews McMeel
PUBLISHING®

Contents

For my inner child.
I hope I am the grown-up
you always needed.

Part 1

Soft

What doesn't kill you, makes you softer

When a vase breaks in Japan, it's glued back together with powdered gold—as if to say, trauma rips you apart, then reassembles you more beautiful.

It's strange how we thank trauma for our strength—as if something good must always come out of suffering, as if being alive isn't an achievement in itself.

Once, at the grocery store, I saw an egg
carton that said, "A little damaged, but
still good."

I am not better or more beautiful than I was
before the trauma. But at my raw, squishy
center, I am still good.

When life cracked me open,
it didn't make me stronger.
It made me softer, messier.
It made me leak all over the
breakfast table.

A well-meaning loved one says, "You are better because of it." I tell them, "Not everything has to be beautiful."

Mount Everest shrunk sixty centimeters after the big quake—600 years of growth, destroyed in a moment.

If something so grand can be struck down by life, what is to become of my small human body?

Why does something good have to emerge from the rubble? Isn't it enough to have emerged at all?

In an alternate universe

We sit in the living room
feeding each other
strawberries.

In this one, I sit
alone, asking the cosmos
to return us to each other,
someplace,
somehow.

The heartbreak guardian

You know the ache that lingers after
heartbreak? I like to think of it as
my guardian.

It sits, legs spread, right on top of my heart,
as if it were a stone in a primordial forest.
I think it's the split that summons it. Those
elf ears prick up at the first sound of pain.

It bares its teeth when I tell it to leave. I
think maybe if I close the crack, it will
disappear with it.

Then, I remember how those trolls from
childhood guarded liminal spaces—like a
bridge between two towns or a cave leading
to a new kingdom.

I think mine guards the space between the
heartbroken and the healed. It won't let
me pass before I'm ready. I need to feel the
pain, the heaviness, first.

The guardian places a gnarly hand on my
shoulder, my night-light shrouding its hairy
face like the moon. It looks at me with big,

yellow eyes, as if to say, "Heartbreak is a thing of nature. It's as predictable as the earthquakes or the receding shoreline.

Be patient. Let it pass. One day it will be gone, and I will be too. Wildflowers will grow over the rock, and you will be soft to touch again.

Be patient. Let it pass. Your time will come soon. But it will not come today."

The first woman to love another woman

The first time I loved a woman,
she lit me up like a soy candle,
which is to say,
the first time
I loved a woman,
I was burning alive.

Flesh and bones
melted down,
built back as a lantern
glowing against her cheek.

And she held me like the first
woman to love another woman,
walking through the woods
in her pilgrim dress.

A lesbian once wrote in
black ink to her lover,
"One day, we'll kiss in
broad daylight.

We'll meet under this tree
when things change,
when it's finally safe."

The leaves ruffle under her skirt
as we shuffle through
the night. This isn't our time.
The world is too young for us.

Her sleeve catches my light,
and we go up in flames,
just like they
wanted us to.

They say the first woman
you ever love
burns right through you.

Perhaps one day,
when the world is older—
when I am older
—we'll rise from the ashes
of the lesbians who
came before us.

One day,
when my heart is
more heart than tinderbox,
I'll meet a woman who turns
my flames back
into flesh.

We'll run through the woods,
sneakers squeaking,
thighs rubbing like skin
instead of matchsticks.

Lips soft, wet.
Faces flushed,
pink as the magnolia growing
on the branches above us.

She'll hold me like the first woman
to ever love another woman,
and also, the very last.

We'll kiss in broad daylight,
the sun glowing orange
on our cheeks.

On multiverses

I no longer think about
all the versions of you
locking eyes with all
the versions of me.

I no longer think about the
infinite Sundays in bed.

Instead, I think of all the
beautiful people I have the
privilege to meet—

all the versions of me who
end up devastatingly
fascinated with people
who aren't you.

If multiverses exist,
there are places in this
universe where you don't
exist at all.

There are places in this
universe where I am happy
without you.

No one realizes the water is toxic because we're too busy filling the cups for the next generation.

The well of generational trauma

My parents drank from the well.
There was no baptism
or ceremony. Where I lived,
the poison was in the water.

I held my breath
as they dunked my head in,
told me to drink,
told me it would be good for me.

Our bloodline is tainted
because well-meaning elders
with loud voices and sharp hands,
never questioned
what they should have.

Grandma worries
about asbestos under the plaster,
when the poison
is in our veins.

Wherever we go,
the trauma of our ancestors
follows. I run anyway—
learn to suck the poison
from my childhood wounds.

I run till my blood runs clear,
till I circle back
to my parents' kitchen table.

I guess it's hard to know
the taste of poison
when you've been
drinking it your whole life.

Mom tells me about the asbestos—
how she thinks it's
why we're all sick.
I say the poison isn't
in the walls,
it's inside us.

But she's too busy filling
the cups of the next
generation to
hear me.

This is what her parents did
and their parents before that.
They drank from the well,
and I did too.

The bitter poison ran
purple down my throat.
But I was lucky—
I got out in time.

I wish I could go back
to save my parents,
to save myself from
my own bloodline.

At least I know
they were victims too.

Their bodies were
simply containers
for the river of poison
we inherited.

They were toxic because
they drank from the well—
not because they
meant to be.

My sister

My sister is light and carefree.
I leave sinkholes in the floorboards.

Sometimes I wish to drop my feelings
on a park bench with a note.

I want to be like my sister.
But my heart is a giant sinkhole.

My tongue bleeds when someone
asks about the weather.

My sister opens her mouth
like a gentle breeze.

My sister is so light,
sometimes I think she'll
float away.

She will tread in and out
of this world
more softly than I will.

Two sets of footprints
running across life's back.

One delicate,
the other, lined in craters.

Both bleeding into
each other in the end.

Dead moths, wishful thinking, and a boy I met on Tinder

I read somewhere that moths use
moonbeams to find their way back to their
nests at night—something to do with their
internal navigation systems.

I pity the lost ones trapped like paper
cutouts in the light fixtures of my
childhood home.

Home is so far from here. I get why the
moths desperately look for it in ten-dollar
light bulbs. I, too, find myself searching
for it in ginger tea and other people's
coat pockets.

The moon hangs like a fluorescent lantern
outside my window, but it's a shade dimmer
than the moon I used to know.

We are standing in an elevator, and I point
at the dead insects in the overhead panels.
You nod, even though I'm not quite sure
you heard me.

But your eyes look familiar, so I let you
craft me wings, only to rip them off with
your fingers later—crouch and make myself
small so I fit in your mason jar.

It's 3 a.m., and we're lying in bed. I press
my ear to your chest like a child snuggled
against the ground, hoping to hear fairies.

Even swathed in harsh light, I fail to see
you for what you are: just a boy in a dirty
sweater, and I, a moth circling a kitchen
lamp it mistakes for the moon.

If a heart breaks
and no one hears it,
did it make a sound?

It's strange how a heart
can break without anyone
ever knowing.

How many hearts shatter
quietly under jackets
on the morning commute,

how many people carry the
shards in their pockets like
loose change?

So much wreckage,
yet nothing to show for it.
No deafening bang,
no colossal echo.

The hum of the radiator
yells louder than
the canyon
in your chest.

What if the heart let out
a scream every time
someone broke it?
Or if the newly single
displayed their bruised
insides behind glass.

People gather to watch
as they crack
in synchrony.

They sound like cymbals,
like temple gongs
going off at the same time.

Like a hundred trees
falling in a sleepy
suburban library.

Like all that pain finally
getting the attention
it deserves.

Where do unrequited feelings go?

I gather every feeling I have
and tell them to go
find her.

She bottles them
in a mason jar
and leaves it
on my windowsill.

When all the parts
of your identity want
a seat at the table...

A bull, a mantis, and a gay girl walk into an Asian restaurant

"How are you?" my great-aunt asks,
pouring tea from a big clay pot. She looks
at me with curiosity; a wall of dim sum
steamers between us.

I want to tell her about the woman who
broke my heart. But I know "How are you?"
means "Tell me how you are in the least
controversial way."

Her chopsticks clink against her bowl, and I
am reminded of how easily it could shatter.
My dad once told me not to be a bull in a
china shop.

"Go delicately; watch where you step."

The Western part of me is screaming. I want
to tear through the table—turn it upside
down with my horns.

This is the part of me that wants chaos and
blood. The part I keep hidden.

My great-aunt pours us more tea, and I
notice the watercolor stems on the pot—
how they're as thin and papery as her veins.

If the bull is let loose, it would tear right
through her.

Go delicately; watch where you step.

"How are you?" she asks. I rein in the
bull, pat its grizzly head. Leaning into
its neck, I whisper, *not every place is
your battleground.*

Here, I must move softly; an Asian mantis
gliding through a china store.

"I've been stressed," I say, without going
into detail. This is my way of being
authentic while causing the least pain.

The bull squirms in its seat. I picture it
charging across the restaurant—shards
of glass in my lap, bloodstains on
the tablecloth.

In a rush of panic, I check on my aunt. The
bull sits quietly in a corner, breathing down
her neck.

Not every place is your battleground.

. . .

And so, we lay our pieces across the table
like carefully chosen mahjong tiles. The
bull smirks.

"This is the only way to make it work," says
Mantis, taking a bite of stir-fried cabbage.

"Can you truly connect without showing
your full self?" asks the bull.

I don't know. But I've been doing it my whole life.

For the multicultural kids

You have a Silly Putty heart
stretched across continents.
And you wonder how far
you can pull it before
it tears.

Part 2

Hungry

What is not mine

If I steal a lover and
turn their tears into *gold*,
does that make me a thief
or an alchemist?

Am I like my aunt,
who picks flowers
from neighbors' gardens?

Am I like my dad,
who plucked my mom
from the home she made
with the first man
she ever loved?

If I am on this earth
because someone had trouble
understanding what wasn't his,
how can I know different?

How can I see something
that grows in someone else's
garden and choose
to walk away?

"Go on," says my aunt,
handing me the kitchen scissors.
The metal cold on my fingers.

I wonder if anyone will notice.
I wonder if you will wear your
gold tears around your neck.

Maybe together we'll steal
all the neighbors' tears—
live in a house where *gold*
piles over the front doorway.

We'll buy all the cherry
blossoms in Tokyo.
And when my aunt arrives
with a pair of scissors
in her pocket,
we'll greet her with
a basket of blooms.

When the younger version of
my dad comes looking
for my mother,
we'll send him off with
directions and a map.

If I am on this earth
because someone had trouble
understanding what wasn't his,
how can I know different?
I don't know any different.

૪ø

The neighbor's daughter sits cross-legged,
admiring her magnolias. She is still smiling
as she runs inside.

My aunt grips the metal scissors
in her shirt pocket, pauses for a
moment, then walks away.

Ant death spirals
and unavailable lovers

They say kids who never felt emotionally
safe become adults who chase unavailable
lovers. We see someone who can't give us
what we need and think we've found home.

The other day, I learned that ants can
walk in circles to their death, following a
familiar scent.

I've lost count of the laps I've run around
the wrong lover. I wonder if the ants know
what's happening. I wonder if their legs
give out just when they think they've
found home.

"Follow me," says my inner child, stretching
out her palm. Her smile is a gaping wound
across her face.

Life will keep sending you the same lessons
until you finally learn them. I think I'm
starting to learn that I have no clue where
home is—but it sure as hell isn't here.

I take her hand, just as she's in the middle of a lap.
"You are enough," I say.

She catches her breath, and for a brief
second, stands completely still.

Letting go

I remind myself to
admire you from afar—
the way you admire a flower
that blooms in someone else's
garden.

Or the great Alps
in all their rugged glory,
that I'll never get to fold
and tuck in my back pocket
to take home.

I tell myself, people
marvel at the grandest mountains,
without ever holding them
in their hands.

You can appreciate beauty
even if it lives a thousand miles
away, or inside the viewfinder
of a rusty old telescope.

I guess I'm just lucky
to bathe in your glow.

I'll let you perch on
my palm
like a monarch butterfly
on a quick
stopover,
before it flies home.

When you want a relationship, but they tell you to "love yourself" instead

Love Yourself
compliments your outfit
but does not want to take it off.
Love Yourself cannot scratch your back,
cannot laugh at your jokes.
Love Yourself takes you to
the other side of the world
but leaves you to watch the sunset
alone.
Love Yourself is
THE party of the year.
Except everyone is too preoccupied
with their phones to dance.
Love Yourself never gets called
on double dates, never serves breakfast in bed.
Love Yourself showers you with gifts
but always exactly what you ask for.
Love Yourself says,
"All the sex in the world won't buy contentment."
Love Yourself forgets to mention that
neither will all the affirmation notebooks.
Love Yourself says freedom is better.
Love Yourself doesn't know if that's true.

Love Yourself is so utterly valuable
but so utterly enraging
when said without a thought.
Love Yourself is life-changing at best,
a Target wall-hanging at worst.
Love Yourself accepts you
exactly as you are,
strokes your hair,
tells you that you're beautiful.
I say, "I already know."

If I were your home

I'd tell you to drop your
baggage at my door.
We'd unpack it together—
put some on a shelf next to mine.
This is a home for all your pieces,
the broken ones too.

I'd tuck your demons in
a shoebox in the attic.
And I swear I won't get mad
if one sneaks out and we
search for hours only to find
it asleep in our bed.

And if this house is too small to fit
the entirety of you,
I'll hang your leaky bits from
the tip of my collarbone.

Then we'll dance in the kitchen
as the kettle boils, singing,
"Bless this home,
bless this home."

Single Girl says,
"I want to fall in love"

World says, "Love yourself,"
like she doesn't already do that,
like it's the answer to everything.

World says,
"You need to GLOW with self-love!"

Single Girl glows with
the fury of a salt lamp.

World says, "You don't need anyone."
Single Girl says, "I want them."

World says, "Love yourself."
Single Girl burns like a store of
slogan candles.
"But I don't feel empowered,"
she says.

World takes out a Sharpie, writes, "Good
things come to those who wait,"
across her body.
Single Girl says,
"How do you know?"

World says, "Love yourself."
Single Girl glows so bright you can
see her from the sky.

People gather to admire her.
She is a beacon of hope,
screaming, "LOOK at me!
I am single!
I am FREE!"

World claps.
From a mile away,
no one notices that
she's on fire.

World says, "Love yourself."
Single Girl wonders why she
still feels sad.

World quotes Jo March
from *Little Women*.

*"I am so sick of people saying that
love is all a woman is fit for."*

Single Girl says, "You missed a line."
Here's what Jo March actually said:

"I am so sick of people saying that love is all a woman is fit for. . . .

But I am so lonely."

The U-Haul truck that never comes

They say a lesbian date
is a U-Haul truck
driving full speed into
the future.

A woman I liked once
deleted all her dating apps
ten days after meeting someone
who wasn't me.

I think my heart is a U-Haul truck,
going over a speed bump
at one hundred miles an hour.

Teetering, swollen—
about to throw up on the
doorstep of the woman
who doesn't want me.

A straight girl once said,
finding your sexuality is a
"beautiful journey."

I tell her it's more like
a dozen U-Hauls, driving
two lanes apart, right
off a cliff.

Maybe my happy ending
isn't a white horse,
or a lesbian Hallmark movie.
Maybe it's just me,
driving alone on the highway,
with the radio on.

Maybe it's the sound of my cat
purring, half-asleep,
on a crumpled sweater.
All the contents of my life,
tinkering softly,
in the backseat.

Sometimes the only way to
stop yourself breaking down,
is knowing you're
the one behind the wheel—

that even when it's hailing and

hope is strapped to
a Styrofoam box,
you'll still remember
how to drive yourself home.

I think the kitchen sink
is a woman

She's so used to cleaning up after people.
We stuff her with cups, spoons, and saucers
stained with peanut butter,
and she cradles it all with open arms.

We pile and we pile.
When she can no longer breathe,
she screams in gushes of water.

All she gets in response
are hands, hands, hands.
Hands washing dishes,
hands washing off the day.

When I am done, I unplug her.
She groans,
and so do I.

Water swirls down the drain.

I feel it running through my fingers,
as if I'm not in my apartment,
but crouched on the shore
feeling the waves trickle
back into the sea.

I think my kitchen sink
wants to be the sea,
free and flowing
instead of a stainless-steel box.

I want to be free and flowing,
but instead, I grab a sponge,
scrub pasta sauce from
the inside of my fork.

Water drips against
the backdrop of the radio.
Like a song
or a heartbeat.

I think my kitchen sink is a woman.
She drips in protest.
She tells me she is the sea.

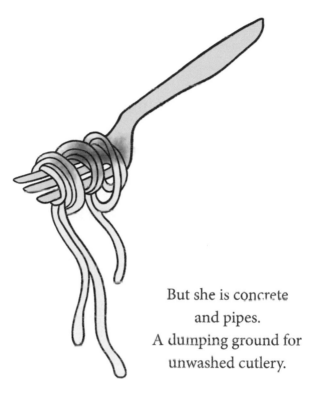

But she is concrete
and pipes.
A dumping ground for
unwashed cutlery.

Just a sink.
Just a woman.

Just like me.

Sourdough and Sunflowers
(on not settling)

My grandma tells me to find a love as steady
and dependable as sourdough.

She sips tea from a dandelion-print mug.
I watch the veins in her neck as she swallows.

৵৹

Gripping a knife, I smear peanut butter
between two slices of bread. Safe but plain,
safe but plain

Sitting at the table is a love that reminds me
of sourdough. It is wholesome and warm.
When you bite into its center, you feel the
grains on your tongue.

It kisses me on the cheek as it leaves for
work, and I wonder if I am ungrateful for
wanting sunflowers, too.

Not just sustenance, but beauty—magic.
I want to sit in a field, raw earth beneath my
toes. I want a love that asks you to reach out
and touch it.

The wind blows in the distance. Sunflowers
sway at my feet. I place my palms on the
warm soil, breathing softly—in and out, in
and out. Safe and full, safe and full.

When I open my eyes, I am back home. The
kitchen counters are cold under my fingers.

Am I naive for wanting sunflowers? Am
I childish? Greedy? Is it stupid to risk
starvation? *Is it stupid to forget the heart can
starve too?*

The sun shines through the kitchen
window. Soap bubbles dance to the ticking
clock. The woman in the reflection looks
hopeful, scared.

As the water fills the basin, I tell her she
deserves both.

*I watch the veins in her neck relax, as
I exhale.*

Part 3

Messy

To a boy I once loved

There is a house I only visit
in my head.
I see us in the kitchen,
planning our future over
flan and coffee.

I see our cream-colored cat,
our purple front door.
Him tending to the plants,
humming some old song.

The garden is blooming,
the sun is warm.
I want to preserve this place
for as long as I can.

Now when I visit,
the sky is overcast,
the purple door, shut.
The flowers we planted
crumble in my hands.

He stands in front of me
with sadness in his shirt pocket.

Asks why I showed him a future
that wasn't real.

I tell him I am sorry—
"That version of the truth
was the only one I had."

I tell him somewhere
in this universe,
we have our house
and cat and garden.

I pull open the curtains
to see him in our kitchen,
discussing travel plans with
a different version of me.

There is love and flan on the table—
sunlight drips from our hair.

*She is everything
I couldn't be.*

All the popular kids are getting married

It's New Year's Eve.
I am eating pâté alone
in a mountain cabin,
while all the happy families
pose in onesies
with their dogs.

I wonder if the rest of my life
will be a series of beautiful places
to see on my own.

My boyfriend wanted to propose
under the stars
in the Dandenong rainforest.
"Pick a ring," he said,
in a small, gentle voice.

All the popular kids
are getting married
and my boyfriend falls
to his knees
as I leave him.

I never got to kiss a girl
under the bleachers in high school.
So, I make up for lost time
with a woman who smells
of incense and cigarettes.

We lean into each other,
waiting for the stars
to fall on our tongues.
But our lips touch
and all I taste is pavement.
For lack of better words,
some things just
suck.

"Pick a ring,"
he said.

And I bought myself
a thousand-dollar ruby,
knowing full well
I had no place to wear it.

By tragic chance,
the first woman I ever kissed
worked at the car parts shop
next door.

So, I ran past the tires and diesel,
head down,
ring on my middle finger.

I wonder how many more
beautiful things
I will see on my own.

Maybe next year
will be different,
or maybe it
just won't.

I adjust my bra in an Uber on the way to a bad date

Classical music plays on the radio
as my driver rubs his balding scalp.
He wears a full suit to drive
people down the block.

I wear a black romper and
a tween girl's bra
to meet someone who could be
the love of my life
or someone I make small talk with
while fighting the urge
to fix my bra.

I've technically stopped wearing
bras. But here I am,
picking at my straps
to the rhythms of Chopin.
Itch, snap, pull,
itch, pull, snap.

It's like the driver has seen this before;
a sanguine guardian angel

carrying girls in ill-fitting bras
to wherever fate wants them.

How many seconds does it take
for someone, somewhere
to watch hope
slip out of their rideshare window?

If you listen closely,
you might hear the orchestra
of sad girls fiddling with their straps
like amateur violinists.

Separate cars, same tune.
Itch, snap, pull,
itch, pull,
snap.

I think we sound like anxiety
mixed with high notes of longing.
I think we mostly sound tired.

Like the feeling of not wanting to
go somewhere,

but doing it anyway,
on the off chance
we find something.

Like mostly finding
nothing at all.

"This is your destination, miss."
I thank him as I step out of the car.
Bra a little more in place,
heart and mind
completely undone.

The vegetarian who keeps girls in jars

I never ate meat around you. Not even at your Christmas party when your entire family had shrimp juice running down their fingers.

You say, "Most people would go vegetarian if they saw the animals in cages." And it's true. Most of us are too afraid to see pain up close.

Is that why you waited months to say you didn't want me? Were you too afraid to see my pain up close?

Years ago, I left a cockroach inside an overturned jar in a hotel room in Marrakesh. Maybe this is karma for my cowardice—a woman who thinks she is too kind to swat my heart with her bare hands.

I think you hoped I'd suffocate quietly.

I think it made you feel kind.

But there is no kindness in leading someone
on because you're too scared to hurt them.
There is nothing kind about the three whole
months I lay in a jar under your bed.

Does the cockroach know that no one
is coming?

Does it know why it's there?

You never told me why you chose her.

You just casually dropped the bomb two
weeks after Christmas. Two weeks after I
slept in your bed.

Honestly, I don't think you're a monster.
Just a child who went too far playing with a
live thing.

"I'm sorry," cries the child, through your
thirty-nine-year-old mouth.

"I should have been better," you say, as you
run from my shaking body.

I hope that when the girl you fall in love
with breaks your heart,

she does it slowly.

I hope she dangles your legs above an
empty pickle jar.

I hope it feels like flying just before
the thud.

The next time someone asks why you're
vegetarian, I hope you picture my
limp body as the word "ethics" rolls off
your tongue.

When you tell people about the animals in
cages—how most people are too afraid to
see pain up close, I hope you know you're
no different.

I think you hoped I'd suffocate quietly.
I think it made you feel kind.
Do you still feel kind?

Conversations with my mother about being gay

My mother tells me I am disgusting
with the same tongue she uses
to tell me she loves me.

She says them both in the same breath.
"I love you."
"Stop hanging around those lesbians."
"Think about the consequences."
"I love you."

What she means is,
"I am scared."
"I don't understand."
"I love you."

She looks down at her palms—
fear washing over her face.
"I love you."
"I love you too," I say.

Home is . . .

. . . the mouth of a great white shark.
My sister polishes its teeth with Windex.
"It's not so bad," she says,
laying a welcome garland
along its tongue.

Home is . . .
a house in a souvenir sand bottle—
calm and picturesque until
it's hanging upside down in a
toddler's fist.

Home is . . .
my mother planting a flower bed
over the rubble,
then standing beside it
in her favorite blue dress.
"It's not so bad," she says.
I say, "It's swallowing me whole."

Home is . . .
an abusive lover
writing to tell me how much
they miss me.
I write back saying,
"I think of you every day."

Home is . . .
my childhood bedroom,
Grandma's curry —
all wrapped in a package
of poison ivy.

Home is . . .
a gentle hand holding on to me
at the airport.
"Go," it says,
loosening its grip on my fingers.
"You're better off without me."

My parents' house

My parents' house is a time capsule
buried deep underground.

The furniture is intact;
my sling bag, a preserved fossil,
exactly where I left it.

At first glance, it looks like
time cannot touch anything here.

Then I notice spots where
the light got in:
new lines on my parents' faces,
Grandma's protruding veins.

It's as if time seeped in
through the gaps and cracked them
at half the speed—

which is to say, my parents' house
is also a time machine.

My family sits in the living room,
flipping through memories
that aren't mine.

Leaving home is taking
rusty kitchen scissors
and cutting your own face
out of the photo albums.

"There's still time to make more,"
says my aunt, placing a hand on my
shoulder. She calls me by the name
I buried in the backyard at eighteen.

There are some things time cannot touch.

My parents' house is a time capsule
and a time machine.

The road that takes me away
carves a new one down my
mother's face.

Her wrinkles run together
as she scrunches her nose—
a map of all the places
she's been without me.

The house calls out from the rear window.
It sits unchanging at the end of the road

till distance swallows it—
a time capsule buried into the horizon.

At first glance, it looks like
time cannot touch anything here.

But it can,
and it does.

My Asian parents asked for Longchamp, but I am a red sequin purse

I can't think of a Longchamp handbag
without picturing an even-tempered Asian
girl strolling down the streets of some
cosmopolitan city.

My dad wants me to be the kind of girl who
carries a Longchamp bag—as straightlaced
as the leather handle dangling from her
wrist, agreeable as a nylon canvas bending
itself to its owner's whims.

Instead, I am a red sequin purse. The kind
with a faux feather trim. The kind you'd see
on a thrift store shelf next to the taxidermy
insects and Wiccan-inspired cookbooks.

An Asian girl with a Rabbit God tattoo
strokes my patchwork fabric, my button
hanging slightly off its thread.

My dad wants me to be a Longchamp bag.

Instead, I am a garish, eccentric thing
hanging flippantly on the arm of the hipster
girl my aunties warned me about.

I am the girl my aunties warned me about.

I laugh to myself as they stretch out their
arms, flaunting their flashy accessories:
Longchamp, LV, Prada, *prospective
doctor children.*

I hear Asian women love Longchamp
because their bags are so light, so practical.

"You can fold them down to the size of
a paperback book!" exclaims an aunty,
placing a hand on the paper-white
shoulders of her son.

I picture her folding him, tucking all his
innate talents inward—till he's the shape of
a neat, flawless medical school acceptance
letter. Or a Longchamp bag trapped under
the weight of her arm.

My dad wants me to be the kind of girl who
carries a Longchamp bag.

By this, he means, I shouldn't take up space.
I should look like everyone else.

I should be expansive enough to fit his
groceries and dreams. Yet as light and
foldable as paper.

By this, he means I should be nothing at all.

Dead factory fabric sitting stiffly on a
conveyor belt, waiting for the stamp of
"good Asian daughter."

Compliant as the quiet girl who carries
it, walking down the streets of some
cosmopolitan city, on the way to fulfilling
someone else's dreams.

Disclaimer:

The quiet Asian girl in the poem is not real.

She is a two-dimensional stereotype of what my
culture wants me to be.

In reality, Asian women are complex and nuanced.

I am complex and nuanced—I am just like the
other girls.

The bridge of bicultural blues

When you are the bridge
between two cultures,
sometimes your back aches
from bending yourself
into a site
of unity.

Earth Girl meets Air

I once met a girl who wore crystals
around her wrist like
creeping ivy.

She was grounded where
I was whimsy—
an Earth Girl to
my Air.

We spent the summer learning
each other's languages.
She gave me her trunk
to lean on.
I blew metaphors in her ear.

That night, I pointed at the
vast kaleidoscope sky.
She couldn't see what I did—
said it all just looked like air.

She reaches out to touch me,
and I float
through the cracks
in her fingers.

Maybe I shouldn't have used
her spine as an anchor.
Maybe I shouldn't have seen
her as my connection to
the ground.

Maybe I was too light
and shifting
next to the elements
she usually held.

I think it ended
simply because
she was Earth and
I am Air.

Our parting was as
natural as the rain.

She tied her shoelaces,
gathered all her trees,
dragged her grand,
tectonic plates
elsewhere.

I look at her again,
before I am pulled in

a new direction by a
gust of wind.

Stroke her face
one last time,
then float away.

One of the girls

I went to a straight girl's PJ party
two months after realizing
I was gay.

The host shows off her cheese platter,
while Olivia Rodrigo sings
about some boy.

She points out everything on the plate:
brie, parmesan,
strawberries,
hummus.

I dip a cracker—
swirl the flavors in my mouth.

I wonder if she'll
look at me the same
if I told her.
Crunch.
I wonder if I'll ever feel
okay

in a crowd of girls.
Swallow.

The truth is,
being gay never felt like
coming home.
It felt more like
getting lost in Oz.

Except,
Oz is the dyke bar,
and I turned up an hour late
in inappropriate footwear.

All I want to do
is run back,
red stilettos clicking,
to a time when I was
"one of the girls."

You see, the sacred thing
about female friendship
is how we hold each other.

How everyone places
their baggage down

and we eat from the
same plate.

I don't know what dish
to bring to the party anymore.

I think my platter looks like:
nail clippers, dyke bar, undercuts,
vagina,

the sheer joy of falling
in love with a woman.
The sheer brutality,

I consider cutting up my sexuality
into bite-sized pieces.
Dousing it in honey so
it goes down softly.

I pray the straight girls
won't wrinkle their noses
or tell me they wish
it was theirs too.

A girl with the kindest
boyfriend
tells me how lucky I am

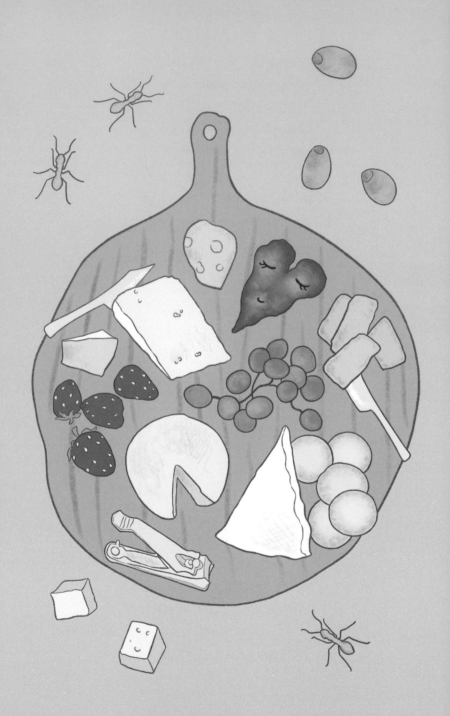

to not have to date men.
"The bar is so low,"
she says,
while he buys her flowers.

I tell her,
the woman I went to
Christmas with
found someone new
by January.

I expect her to hold my pain.
But she just looks confused.

I want to be
"one of the girls,"
crying over some boy.

Because then,
when I put my crumpled heart
on the shared platter,
there'll be someone to
put her hand on my shoulder
and say, "Me too."

I've now gone twenty-eight days . . .

. . . without thinking about
the curve of your
shoulder blade.

—is this what healing is?

Part 4

Swallowed

Hot Girl vs. Slasher Film

Hot Girl walks on screen
in tight denim shorts.
The male characters leer.
The audience leers with them.

She goes for a swim
in her tiniest bikini.
By nightfall,
she squeezes the water
from her hair—
fucks a lifeguard
in the teal blue lake.

Then, she heads to the cabin,
wet swim bottoms
dripping water
onto the windowsill.

She thinks she's alone
but the killer is near—
infuriated by the scent
of a free woman.

He sneaks up from behind,
grabs her by the hair—
wants to teach her
what the world thinks
of women like her.

Hot Girl screams.
The audience smirks.
The killer says
she punches
like a girl.

She pulls a knife from her
bra and slits his throat.

The killer falls backward—
. . . *thud*, *crash* . . .

then silence.

The audience is confused.
No one says a word,
until one girl claps,
then another.

Suddenly the whole crowd
is cheering.

I am not Buffy the Vampire Slayer

Buffy was sixteen,
blonde, doe-eyed—

which is to say,
those writers took the most
consumable girl and made
her a stake-wielding hero.

Pried her out of America's jaws,
so she could stand for
all of us. Fight for all of us.
Except, she is not one of us.

She is a projection of
the girls who walk
with keys
cutting into their palms.

The girls who never
stood a chance.

The truth is, the world
is a dangerous place
for girls like us.

On TV, bad people
turn out to be demons
defeated with a spell or kick.

The demons in real life
always turn out to be
people—

a clingy ex,
a shadowy man
walking a little too close.

They say the scariest part
of Buffy was when she faced
those skeletal figures with
metallic teeth.

I think the scariest part
was the episode where
she loses her powers
and has to walk home
alone.

Which is to say,
the scariest monster
is a boy

asking for a lap dance
in a dark alleyway.

Which is to say,
without her powers,
she is just a girl.
And the alleyway
is a strange man's throat.

Buffy eventually gets her
powers back. Flips her
hair and turns the next
monster into dust.

But the truth is,
she is not one of us.
No matter how much
we want her to be.

The truth is,
if a normal girl
was cornered at the end
of a dark alley,
she wouldn't be able to
throw a sassy punchline
and make the monster

disappear.

'The truth is,
in the real world,
she dies.

Good Girls

They warn you so much
about the night,
it'll be your fault
if you slip out
and end up swallowed
by it.

This is the only place
you'll be safe.

So, hush, little girl—
settle into your cage.

Listen to your mom's
soft voice:
"You are safe here,
you are safe."

Am I to blame if I walk into the mouth of a bear?

I am eighteen, in the home
of a boy I barely know.

We drink from paper cups,
and I lean on his arm.
Count the cracks in the ceiling
like I'm counting stars.

"Look at this," he says.
And he scales a creaky ladder.
Big, pointy lamp in hand
like he's about to hang a lantern
from a thousand-year-old
oak tree.

We sit under its glow.
King and queen of an empire
the size of an IKEA rug.

He offers a hand,
crafts me a throne
from his spine,
and I am now in his bedroom.
The air here is cold,
and his sheets stretch like

a desert skyline.
I feel uneasy traveling this far.

I would have preferred to stay
in his kitchen with the paper cups
and all those stars.

But I am eighteen—
scared to expose
the child inside.

I was so desperate to paint him
as this sweet boy,
I somehow missed all the bones
beneath the sheets.

Am I to blame for entering this land?
Can I call myself a victim
when I walked right into the
mouth of a bear?

"It's all a mirage, dear,"
the sky seemed to say.

So, I ignored the fangs,
wandered the sands
calling the boy's name.

And just like that,
the bear pounced.

I once read that if you're
attacked by a bear,
you should close your eyes
and play dead.

So, I waited for it to pass
like a comet
or a desert storm.

Counted the cracks
in the ceiling like
I was counting stars.

When the feast is over,
the boy returns.
He walks me out of the desert,
then offers to drive me home.

In the front seat of his car,
his fangs fold into molars,
and the beast shrinks
till it fits into a cotton T-shirt.

My best friend asks about my date
and I tell her about the boy,
not the bear.

And the next morning,

I call him, as if the desert
was never real.

Best friend, I am sorry for being
too afraid to tell you the truth.
Fellow sisters, I am sorry
for trying to mold a bear
into a boy.

And I am sorry,
little girl,
still buried in the sand.

Tonight, I light a candle
and say a prayer,
just for you.

When I see my rapist's baby photo on Facebook

I want to reach into the screen
and snap its neck.

Am I a monster for wanting to kill
a soft, smiling thing?

What if,
twenty-eight years later,
the soft, smiling thing
grows fangs?

If you see a nest of black widow eggs,
are you morally obligated
to squish them
before they crawl into the
bed of some poor,
unsuspecting girl?

I picture the spider,
crawling by itself
on the side of my arm.

I think about squishing it.

I think of its juices
running down my fingers.

Then I trap it in a jar,
hold it up to the light,
before letting it go.

Stale fruit and
hand-me-down sexism

My grandma pulls an apple
from her shopping bag,
clean and wrapped
in cling wrap.

"So, the flies don't get it,"
she says, biting into its flesh
like a lady.

Her mouth, small and quiet.
Legs, clean and wrapped
in a cotton skirt.

She glances at my mom's
bare ones,
hands her social conditioning
like a piece of fruit.

I watch her add a sprinkle of sugar
before taking a bite.
A new meal with the same
core ingredients:
be pretty,

be a lady,
be small,
be quiet,
be good.

She hands me a spoonful.
Slowly, I become the fruit shaper.
Slowly, I become
the fruit itself.

The sun shines on my soft skin
as I sit in a basket at the grocery store.
There are so many hands
poking and prodding.
So many mouths.

The flies gather around my ripe,
exposed flesh.
The men are starving.

My mom and grandma appear,
shopping bags draped
over their arms.

They pick me from the bunch
as if I am a prized apple,
wrap me in cling wrap and

take me home.

My grandma inspects me in
the sunlight.
I hear my mom telling her
I'm beautiful.

She pulls a knife from the drawer,
carves me slowly,
cautiously, lovingly.
My sweet flesh,
sprinkled with cinnamon.

I smell clean. I smell good.
Just in time—
the men are starving.

To the men on the street who shout "ni hao"

You arrive at my border line,
compass in pocket.

For I am foreign land,
and you are a thirsty voyager,
dividing my flesh into countries
with dirty fingernails.

You stick flags along my spine,
for you seek a China doll.

All the while forgetting
I am five feet of flesh and bone.

But you don't see skin,
you see origami paper.

And those fingers,
they're aching to fold me—
slice me in
half with
that tongue.

Slice me like meat
on a plate,
legs spread like
chopsticks.

Chop up my limbs.
Stuff 'em in a plastic bag.
Thank you,
come again!

I am a lovely dumpling girl
curtsying behind
take-out box walls,
and you eat me with a fork,
doused in soy sauce
and ignorance.

But what you'll find is
I taste like opinions.
I'll drown you in the ocean
between my legs.

I pity the men
who wash up on my shores,
mistaking me for lands
that promise

floral fans and
mandarin orange summers,

when what I am is a woman—
nothing more,
nothing less.

Women are not candy bars . . .

. . . that lose value
once their wrappers
come off.

Part 5

New

Girl goes to sleep and wakes up thirty in the movies

Everyone laughs, even though
that's how it's always been.

I blink and I am sixteen,
then eighteen,
then twenty-two,
renting an apartment in the city.

Twenty-two looks so glamorous
from afar. A pretty silhouette
in a high-rise window.

So grown-up in a black dress,
until you see her use
her finger as a butter knife.

Twenty-two sheds her sparkly eye shadow,
her little black dress.

Now she's twenty-six,
laughing at how grown
she thought she'd be
by now.

All the while thinking
the same of thirty.

I don't think we ever grow up.
We're just bigger kids
with better clothes.
Forever little girls playing
dress up for our future selves.

The more you shed,
the more you realize,
it's always been you
standing naked in front
of the mirror.

I want to wake up
on my thirtieth birthday
and greet the woman I see.
But also, all the women
I've been.

Because when you're thirty,
you're also twenty-six, and twenty-two, and eighteen,
and sixteen, and eight.

That's how it is.
That's how it's always been.

Mount Fuji isn't lilac up close

Take me back to Fuji,
to that deserted motel
with rusty pink boats.

To that first rainy night—
wet socks and honey chips.
The stillness of the world.

I asked you why Fuji glowed lilac
from a distance, when up close,
it's dull and gray. Rough edges
marking my fingertips.

You say something about
light refractions. I say,
"All the postcards were lying."

Maybe Fuji was a metaphor
for the future—
so enticing from afar.

So full of hope and mysticism,
when you're sitting on tatami mats
in the warmth, sipping tea.

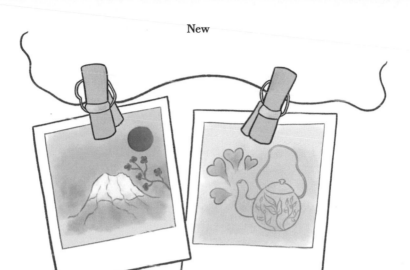

I wish I could crystallize that moment.
Freeze-dry and hang it above my bed.

At least I'll know there's a place where
things felt simple. A place where
the only thing we ran from
was the rain.

My mind still goes back to Fuji,
to that night in the motel
with the chips and tatami mats.

And us,
frozen like a postcard,
shimmering
and so far away.

I picture her as a flower tree

When my great-aunt died,
the bougainvillea tree
outside her house
bloomed for the first time
in years.

We'd never seen
so many white flowers.

My dad said she was sending
a message. I shrug,
not quite sure I believe in
the great beyond.

But I like seeing her as
something alive,
something growing.

I picture her as the tree—
leaves outstretched,
green.

And I think,
if she is the tree,
she is also the soil

nourishing its roots.
She is the ants,
and the early morning dew.

If she is the tree,
she is also the birds,
the stray twigs,
the wind under their wings.

She is the soft, vapory clouds.
She is the sky itself.

She is the rich, throbbing
fullness of the human experience,
and also, nothing at all.

She is love
and suffering
and pain
and loss
and beauty.

She is the whole world.
She is her small house
in her small town.

She is her favorite dried plums,
a gold bangle on her dresser,
a pot of rice,
a bougainvillea tree,

this poem.

Lessons from the sun

She stands there,
whole and glowing.

I watch the universe
stroke her warm back,
then crack it
like a yolk.

I watch her bleed
all over town.

She says she's done this before,
a billion times.
She says the highs and lows
are just part of life.

She tells me that
when it is my turn,
I must feel it all.
I must surrender.

"Watch me," says the sun,
and we walk hand in hand
through the pain,
through the bleeding.

All I see is gold.
So much gold.

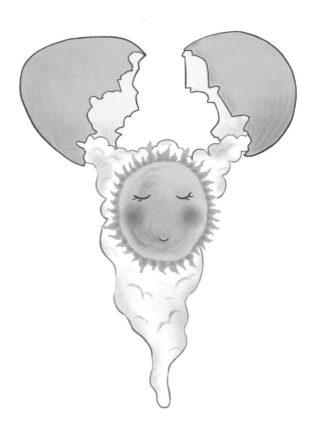

Lessons from my plantar wart

I once got this vile plantar wart
that hurt like a bitch.

I thought it would stay on my toe forever.
I'd done the grieving,
accepted my fate.
My mind loves
a worst-case scenario.

I spend so much time
thinking of what could go wrong,
that for once,
I hold on to
what didn't.

I arrange each fear on my desk
the way people
arrange photo frames.

They look like:

1. All the planes I didn't die on

2. All the escalators too

3. Mosquito bites that turned out
        to be mosquito bites

    4.   My parents alive
on the other end of the phone

5.   The candles that didn't catch fire

    6.   My plantar wart
fallen off on the kitchen floor

I line up these moments like
    trinkets of my survival.

They tell me,
my mind is smart,
but it can't always be trusted.

That maybe things will
be okay.

That one day, I might find
whatever hard thing I'm going through,
defeated on the kitchen floor
when I least expect it.

That no matter the turbulence,
the plane is
most likely to land
on the other side.

That sometimes
you gotta sit tight
and watch a trashy movie,

because if the worst is
going to happen,
there's nothing I can do
to stop it.

And the worst
is not going to happen
just because my mind
says it will.

The little gay girl
I carried inside me

My mother is the kind of woman
who keeps a spotless home:
weeds plucked, laundry folded,
shoes out of sight.

So, when I was six years old,
she put on her rubber gloves—
tucked my gay parts inside of me
like she was clearing away
stained dishes.

And I grew up "straight,"
unaware of the little gay girl
I carried in my belly.

All the while,
she did not die.
She simply grew inward,
like a droopy plant
sitting in the shade.

Sometimes, she
pressed her
cheek to my skin.
Other times, I felt
her scratching
inside me.

She eavesdropped on
high school sleepovers
and conversations about boys.

When I had my first kiss,
she made herself so small
she nearly vanished
completely.

Then one day,
after she'd been asleep
for so long,
I met you.

My little gay girl glowed
through my skin,
and for the first time,
I saw her.

She morphed into a dozen candles
and my body,
once vast and rolling,
folded itself into a flimsy
lantern shell.

"Use your light
to find your way home,"
you whispered.

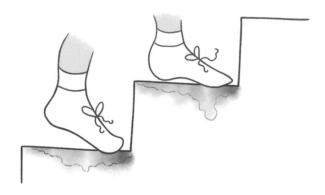

And when she was too scared
to climb out on her own,
you went down there with her.

Held her hand and told her
she didn't need to stay
a ghost.

Last month, I saw my mother
at a family dinner.
My little gay girl,
now tall and blooming
from all the sunlight on her skin.

My mother recoils at her sight—
curls her lip
and calls her disgusting.
Attempts to send her
back into my rib cage

so she can shut the door
for good.

But my little gay girl stays put,
her sun-drenched limbs
stretched across the table.

In this light, my mother
doesn't look frightening—
and my little gay girl
is now a woman.

She looks her in the eye,
tosses her hair,
and laughs.

New Year and Old Year
are in an age gap relationship

Old Year and New Year
are sitting in a bar.
New Year scarfs down a burger
like she's eating for the first time.
Old Year laughs.

New Year smells of hope
and pink champagne.
Old Year smells like
last Thursday's office commute.

New Year wants to
run in the snow,
tongue out,
tasting everything.
Old Year's back aches.

New Year has skin like
a blank canvas.
Old Year's face is marked with
all the places he's been.

He has a life plotted out—
a house, a car, a dog.
New Year is a mysterious secret,
asking to be unfurled.

"Unravel me," she says.
Placing her fingers over
her hidden months.

Old Year expects to discover magic.
Finds all the same
predictable things
in its place

Depression as a Pinterest quote

On my worst days,
I spent so much time with
my head under the covers.

The darkness felt safe—
like how it must feel
to be buried.

I slept underground for months.
Till the duvet hardened,
and a layer of moss spilled
over the side of the bed.

Then slowly,
over time,
I felt more seed
than corpse.

Someone once told me,
"You are not buried,
you are planted."
I hate affirmation quotes,
but I grabbed this one

like a rope.

If life has taught
me anything,
it's that from pain,
comes change.

And the thing about change
is that it hurts
so fucking
much.

There's violence in sprouting.
The new always tears
through the softness
of what came before.

What doesn't kill you,
doesn't make you stronger.

It makes you a sapling
that grew through barbed wire—

bent, misshapen,
maybe a little ugly.

I guess my bed was always
a cocoon. And those sheets
were not a shroud,
but a house,
spun of fine silk.

I poke my finger into the
outside world. I don't know
if I am better or more beautiful.

I just feel alive.
I just feel
new.

A love note for you

You have reached the
end of this book.

Thank you for visiting
my museum of feelings.
Thank you for wandering
here with gentle feet.

I hope you leave more tender.
Here is your coat on the way out.

I would be nothing without you.
So, thank you
for making a poet
out of a girl.

I hope you sit with
your darkness
the way you sit with the
night sky.

I hope you process it all.
I hope you remember
sunlight exists, too.

I accept you exactly as you are.
All your dark parts
are safe with me.

Index

Anti-Acknowl-edgments

"Artists are too stupid to do anything else."

—That's what my dad always told me.

I was nearly too afraid to be a "useless artist." In another life, I'm still at my full-time corporate job. I'm still the daughter he always wanted.

This book would not be here without my self-belief.

So, thank you, Past Self. Thank you for knowing we could be more. Thank you for continuing to trust that we will make it— even though we're not quite there yet.

And thank you to my audience—for showing me that I'm not alone with my big, squishy feelings. Thank you for every single comment, DM, and share. They all carried me here, one by one.

Even if I never make it, thanks for giving me the courage to try.

About the Author

Suri Chan—known for the popular Instagram account @poemsbysuri—is a prize-winning poet. She speaks to women, the queer Asian community, and anyone with big feelings.

Suri is a migrant from a long line of migrants. Her work is inspired by her ancestors. The ones who created food that tasted like home with the herbs of their new land. Their ingredients were simple: nuts, shredded veggies, and sweet sauce. But the resulting meal was always grand.

Suri likes to think she does the same with everyday words.

Follow Suri on social media for new
poems and relatable life takes:

Instagram: @poemsbysuri

TikTok: @surichanpoet

Andrews McMeel Publishing
a division of Andrews McMeel Universal
1130 Walnut Street, Kansas City, Missouri 64106
www.andrewsmcmeel.com

24 25 26 27 28 SDB 10 9 8 7 6 5 4 3 2 1

ISBN: 978-1-5248-9224-1

Library of Congress Control Number: 2023948229

Editor: Danys Mares
Art Director/Designer: Diane Marsh
Production Editor: Jasmine Lim
Production Manager: Julie Skalla

Cover design and illustration by: Eva Polakovičová
Interior illustrations by: Suri Chan
Large salad bowl illustration on page 71 drawn
from a tutorial at helloarsty.com.
Bottom salad plate on page 71 drawn from a
licensed Masterfile Royalty Free image.
Quote on page 49 from *Little Women* (2019).

ATTENTION: SCHOOLS AND BUSINESSES
Andrews McMeel books are available at quantity discounts with
bulk purchase for educational, business, or sales promotional use.
For information, please e-mail the Andrews McMeel Publishing
Special Sales Department: sales@amuniversal.com